THE PERKS OF A K-FANGIRL

SIMRAN KAUR

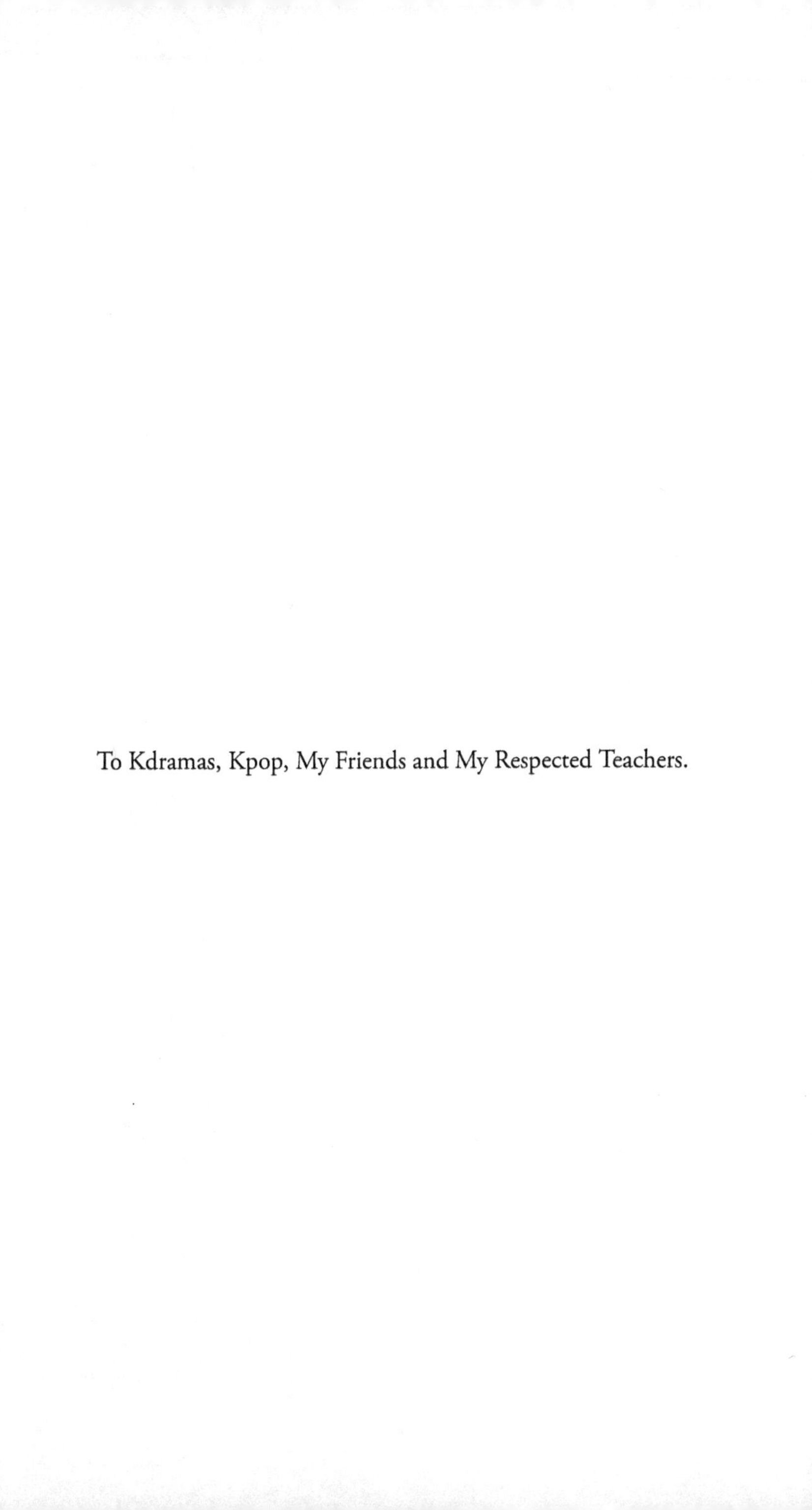

To Kdramas, Kpop, My Friends and My Respected Teachers.

Contents

Contents

Contents

Disclaimer

The following poems may contain references to Kpop Artists, Kdramas, Songs, Musicians, Singers, Literary Figures, and real-life people. These have been mentioned as a tribute and an inspiration, and to express gratitude; to announce how they have helped me be me.

Any or every name, title or work mentioned remain the property of their own copyright holders. I do not own anything except my feelings that turned into this collection of poetry.

There may be some use of explicit language. Reader discretion advised.

I am merely a "fan" of any or every name, title or work mentioned in this poem. My only wish is for this to reach the ones who gave me the chance to recognise me, so that they feel my gratitude.

Foreword

"Begin writing here" is what I am seeing. I don't know where to begin; and this is actually what I write in the beginning of every single one of my writing piece- chats, letters, messages, posts, etc. Thankfully, I didn't do this with the countless answers I wrote during my exams. Otherwise, I wouldn't be here.

This book reflects my inner journey that holds chaos, a yearning for warmth, blessings in disguise and much more. I wrote these poems for me whenever I felt sad or had "Eureka" moment about life. Some just contain utter gratitude for my friends. A few are filled with respect for my teachers who brought me to my virtue of writing. Few of them have my thoughts for my favourite Korean People, hence the title; for I am truly a Fangirl in all its aspects.

The poems that you will come across in this book will represent my inner havoc with the hint of my emotion.

Preface

"Talking" certainly isn't my strong point. Well, this book in itself will do a lot of talking; I hope, on my behalf. I'll also muster some courage and begin.

This book is a collection of my poems that I wrote at various different points in time. As a birthday gift for my friends, to wish my teachers- 'Happy Teacher's Day', a form of greeting and expressing my utmost gratitude; the feelings were there, words came, lines formed and I had literal poems in front of me. I am a big fan of music and I definitely had songs on most of the time I wrote these poems- some of them which you would really find a mention of. Songs are my biggest inspiration. My feelings are my supporters and the intent in writing these poems. Since the feelings were being too much, they came out this way.

I started writing my poems on the day I had a realisation. A realisation that I have only me to talk to now. The one I trusted with my words wasn't interested anymore. Whenever I had something to talk about: a song, a scene, a movie, a day, a feeling, a diagnosis, or something that makes up my life; I wrote a poem. The poems helped me vent out the feelings building up inside me.

What helped me actually write and express were the numerous kpop songs I've heard till now- the result of being a 'multi-stan', the countless kdramas I've been watching since 2017; along with the nature and our beautiful universe.

My feelings became my gateway to write these poems. The tormenting feeling when your own family treats you like a 'tissue' to use and throw. The blissful and overwhelming feeling when your kpop idols and kdrama actors love you to the moon and beyond, no matter if they know you or not. The amazing feeling when you are appreciated by your teachers, and you follow their footsteps in life. The feeling that your true friends give you- that can't be described, because how can you describe the love and understanding they give you which your own family failed to give you. The feeling of belongingness that comes while watching a korean drama that you can escape into. The child-like feeling when you endulge into children movies, books and shows. All these feelings gave me words that you would be reading ahead.

My collection of poems is for every person who ever felt unheard, unloved, lonely, dispirited, discouraged and lost in life; and they were pulled into light and happiness by their true friends, classes, teachers, moments of 'me-time', kpop songs, the people who sang those songs, different movies, korean dramas (they help me go by, everyday); and much more.

I am a big "fan" of kdramas and kpop. They have helped me escape into a world that's totally mine because I am considered something there, of some worth. In reality, I am actually nowhere (except ofcourse in some really good people's life, so all of you good people, shush!). If I start talking about my "fangirling", it would take a larger space than my poems. So, I will just say,"Because I have kpop, kdramas and various other cinematic universes and nature itself, I am here. Those are my perks."

Acknowledgements

I would like to extend my heartiest gratitude to all the people in my life—without whom, I wouldn't be here today.

To all my friends, thank you for always supporting me, no matter what.

To my respected teachers, who have appreciated me not only as their student but also as a good human being—your faith has meant a lot.

To my favourite Koreans—your art and warmth have made me feel worthy of the life I live.

To music, movies, and nature—for helping me flow through life with a little more ease and grace.

Lastly, a big "thank you" to everyone who will read this collection. Your contribution—your time, your presence—means the world to me.

Prologue

Air Vent

Saw in a kdrama once.

How they expressed,

The internal struggle,

The overwhelming emotions,

Found a way, they did.

An air-vent!

They screamed and screamed,

Until their lungs gave out.

Wanted a way out,

I found that notebook,

That holds my feelings.

In the form of poems,

My air-vent!

Because of a kdrama,

For a teacher,

For a friend,

For my kpop idols,

All to express!

1. "Now The Time Feels Right"

Now the time feels right,
No other way left
I pick up this notebook,
With a pencil in my hand.

Is it the journey of the notebook,
I pour my inner self in?
Is it the journey of this pencil?
Or of Ed Sheeran"s voice in my ears?

'Tis unknown.
Words just appear now,
Turning the gears in my brain.
Now the time feels right, Oh!

"Ed Sheeran is an English Singer. I am a fan of his music and he inspired me to form these lines. It is a fan poem with no copyright infringement intended."

2. "How Is It The Reader?"

How is it so?
Reader in me,
Prevalent since childhood.

The school library books,
Read in a day, a two,
Some found me with late fine receipts.

English Literature Book Stories,
My aid in free periods,
And a smile on my face.

Oh, the start of Harry Potter era,
A world to escape in,
Being magic myself.

Teenage filled with Chetan Bhagat,
Grateful to the one who set my journey,
I'm onto Shakespeare, Yeats, Chaucer.

"'Harry Potter' is one of my favourite series by J.K. Rowling, and they built my road as a reader, and now, writer. I am truly a fan of Harry Potter and thus, couldn't help mentioning them. I wrote this as a fan, no copyright infringement intended."

"'Chetan Bhagat' is a Contemporary Indian Author. I have read all his works, he truly gave me what I needed, through his books. As his reader, I couldn't help mentioning him. No copyright infringement intended."

"William Shakespeare, W.B. Yeats, Geoffrey Chaucer, they are the writers I read day and night about, during my Masters. Their works gave me the words I have today, thus, they had to be mentioned. No copyright infringement intended."

3. "How Is It The Writer?"

How is it so?
Writer in me,
Lost till now.

For my best friend,
Another amazing friend,
My beloved Korean singer.
I say with a giggle,
"For teacher, still in thoughts."

A dramatic monologue?
Free Verse?
'Tis for you to know.

This is my world
This is an escape
Let's make life "POETICAL".

4. "Can I Live?"

Was it Midnight?
Was it Dawn?
The loneliness crept in.

Now, it's every moment.
Alone in the classroom,
Sitting with my family,
For whom I don't exist
Unless, for criticism.

The busy friends,
The 'zero-understanding' family,
The wet eyes are more regular now.

Love and Relationship not allowed,
No major life decisions allowed,
No acceptance of what you want,
Is living allowed?

Can I live?
Is it okay to live?
Is it okay to be happy?

5. "Yes, I Can"

'Twas morning,
Peace in the afternoon,
Felt the loneliness subsiding,
Light crept in.
Only for short moments,
With my classmates,
In my room,
Where my world is,
I live with laughter.
Friends like family,
Numerous Korean Singers and Actors,
Fast heartbeat and blushing,
Regular Now.
Love from friends and my teachers,
The decision of no-hesitance now,
The need for acceptance vanishes,
Every moment I live.

Yes, I can live.
With a pretty smile on my face.

6. "Sunshine"

The clouds swept in,
No ray of Sunshine.

Late-night binge watching,
Shedding tears for a while.

Tightly cuddling my teddy,
Fills for the daily need of-
"Maybe just one hug, please!"

Sunshine covered my drapes,
Once I was exhausted enough to sleep.

The long hours of sleep,
Found a sunny day,
With clouds still looming above.

7. "My Catharsis"

XOXO, on in my ears
His voice resonating
Through my earphones.

Third episode of 'The Glory'
I ask myself:
"Why watch such cruelty?"
It felt cathartic.

Revenge? Your own family?
Impossible!
Too kind for this world,
Dramas are my catharsis

My answer, if you ask-
"Why those dramas daily?"

"'XOXO' is a song by EXO, a South Korean-Chinese Kpop band. 'The Glory' is a Korean Drama. I am a kpop fan and kdrama fan, thus, they became a part of me and my poem. This is a fan poem. No copyright infringement intended."

8. "You"

You being there for me,
Taking me in your arms,
Your soothing touch,
The caress on my head.

In times of need,
You come like the sunrise,
And the darkness is no more,
With you by my side.

You, who I can talk to,
You, who lights up my life,
You, who makes my lips curl upwards,
You, the protector of my life.
Now, I question- "Who is 'you'?"

9. "Red Lights"

"The moment when I close my eyes,
All I see is Red Lights."
Swollen Thumb, Bruised Hand
But a big smile and bliss,
On my face.
The Routines, The Patterns,
The PIN, The Playlists,
The Songs, The Voices,
The decorator in me.
Everything's back,
So is my light!

Corners of my mouth curled up,
"Red Lights" is my all-time favourite.

"'Red Lights' is a song by South Korean Kpop Band, 'STRAY KIDS'. The quoted line is from the same song. I am their fan. The song gave me happiness, inspiration and energy to write this poem. This is a fan poem. No copyright infringement intended."

10. "Daughter's Day"

'Twas Daughter's Day today,
Not in anyone's memory here.

Some moment, Some memories,
Always there.

A question here: "Why always children?"
Children need to be grateful to you.
Why not you?

Happy to bring us here,
Why not let us be happy too?

Nothing much,
Just your hugs,
Some credit,
Some worth,
And, simply your warmth.

All that purely on Daughter's Day,
Why can't you be grateful too?

11. "Turbulence"

Darkest of Times,
Curtain in front of my eyes,
The melody flowing through my body,
In my darkest times.

The blooming flowers in my bedsheet,
Solace in my room,
With the Air-Conditioner Cooling my body,
Hope in my heart,
Cool down my burning body!

A Few Hours more,
A Few Days more,
Will it really arrive?
The Tool that stays a long time,
Calming the TURBULENCE in me.

12. "Tears Of The Night"

Tears welling up in my eyes,

Noone around me,

Strength slowly dissipating,

Sleep should be natural,

For I wann dream you,

For I know,

Then, I will gain the strength.

The strength to survive, ALONE!

13. "Poetry"

Lines after lines,
Words after words,
This is the way.

Now, that feeling,
I am not alone!
New Found Passion- Poetry, My Friend!

Filling up the space,
Left empty by some homosepians,
Giggling at the thought of it,
I can sleep well.

Back to my playlist, please.....

14. "Moments"

Something unbearable,
Something special.
Life goes on,
With nothing but moments....

Moments to leave behind,
Moments to forget,
Moments to cherish,
Moments to love,
Moments to live....

"I will never make you lonely...."
In your voice,
'Tis all the assurance
I ever want.

15. "Wolfchan"

Your Big Hug,
That Big Smile,
Those words,
All the comfort I need.

The Tears in your eyes,
Your screams that-
Enunciate 'Protection',
All the care I need.

"'Wolfchan' is the name of Bangchan's character in SKZoo collection of respective Stray Kids members' characters. I wanted to thank Bangchan for everything, from Stray Kids, for his love for his fans. I am a huge fan of his. This poem is my 'thanks' to him, a fan poem. No copyright infringement intended."

16. "A Star Faraway"

Jealous?-
Maybe, But a lot more Happy.

Your warm words
And, my tears.
Miss you more,
That's all I wanna say.

A star faraway,
Happy to live-
On the same Earth,
In the same time,
WITH YOU!

17. "'Cause It Was You"

Time slipped by,
Like water flowing down,
All 'cause it was you,
My friend- my most beautiful woorld!

Ah, wait! 'Tis 'Best Friend' now,
Always there when desired,
The movie, the icecream,
The heart-rending moments,
Turned to feeling worth-it,
Worth-it of the life I live,
All 'cause it was you,
My best friend- my closest person!

All I have is gratitude,
For the way you show up,
Everytime, like my saviour,
I grow, learn, laugh, sing, VIBE!
All 'cause it was you,
My dearest- my miraculous happening!

18. "You And The Letter Read"

The soft melody in my ears,
Your soft voice,
My heart beating softly,
Time slips by,
Yet, All I have is memories.

The roaring firecrackers outside,
The BOOM sound,
My eyes awaiting the view,
Time slips by,
Yet, All I have is memories.

Your beautiful way,
To tell me,
"Yeah, I read your letter."
Me dancing on my bed,
Seeing you read it,
Oh, the blooming happiness in my heart!

19. "When You Read The Letter"

I was casually scrolling,
But you made it so special,
You appeared on the screen,
Holding a bunch of pages,
The caption said-
You are reading a letter,
The next second-
I repeat the video,
It struck me,
"YOU ARE READING MY LETTER!"
Noone else folds it that way,
Noone else gives it that way,
Noone else says that much,
I recognise the sheets,
I recognise the folds,
I check and re-check,
I read and re-read,
The letter I sent-
Saved on my PC!
My body moves on its own accord,
Playing your record,
For days!

20. "Leave"

Stray Kids' "LEAVE",
Rings in my ears,
Such a sweet melody,
Like a healing,
That's what I'm feeling!

The things I want to leave-
The hesitation, the overthinking,
The things that pull me down.
That's enough, now no more,
That's what I'm feeling!

To my pain, To my sorrow,
To my loneliness,
I want you to leave,
I want to be free from you,
That's what I'm feeling!

"'Leave' is a song by South Korean Kpop Band, 'STRAY KIDS'. The song touched my heart more than ever and inspired me. I am their fan and this is a fan poem. No copyright infringement intended."

21. "Book Fair"

Today and tomorrow,
A Book Fair!
I really wanna go,
What do I do?
Noone to go with!
But I don't wanna-
loose the chance!
To get more books,
To look at more books,
To maybe get more of-
HARRY POTTER ORIGINALS!
I say-
LET'S GO TOMORROW!!
YEAH!!

❧❧❧

"'Harry Potter' is one of my favourite series by J.K. Rowling, and they built my road as a reader, and now, writer. I am truly a fan of Harry Potter and thus, couldn't help mentioning them. I wrote this as a fan, no copyright infringement intended."

22. "Red Bean Jelly"

A new vibe-
Never heard BIBI this way,
Brand New melody that heals,
Sweet Red Bean Jelly,
Childhood memories come up,
Days go by,
A little sugar rush,
Like those texts from-
Friends who care a lot.

"BIBI is a South Korean singer who has inspired so many all over the world, one of them being me. 'Red Bean Jelly' is actually the English translation of the title of one of her songs. I was mesmerised by it and thus, this poem was created. This is a fan poem. No copyright infringement intended."

23. "This Is Our Happy Place"

'This Is Our Happy Place'.
That's the postcard..
I picked up at the fest.

Ah, the fest- LIBERATION,
Giggling at the thought,
I reminisce- the games,
the icecream, the cute bites!
No stopping,
No hesitance,
No resistance,
Only peace and MY happiness!

'This Is Our Happy Place',
That's the postcard..
I picked up at the fest:
Thinking of you,
Thinking of us,
You and me together!

24. "Conviction Of Nothing"

The Conviction,
'Tis gonna be this way,
'Tis permanent.

Change is permanent,
But it definitely isn't,
'Tis struggling.

Survival of the fittest,
That's it now,
To live now,
YOU HAVE NOTHING!

25. "Conviction Of Everything"

The Conviction,
I'll go my way,
'Tis my life.

Life's changing,
But it doesn't stop,
'Tis balancing.

Living to the fullest,
You have it all,
To survive now,
YOU HAVE EVERYTHING!

26. "Family Path"

Oh, I was finally over it.
I could finally breathe,
But here it comes again,
Choking me tighter and tighter-
The Ridicule, The Disgust,
The Jealousy, The Hatred....
What do I do now?
What do you want from me?
To end it all,
Shall I end me?
Not just y'all, My closest one too...
Well, there's been a relief with her atleast.
I thought I needed her,
When you made me walk on this path,
But all I needed was to pick up this
notebook again....
No continuity with one who doesn't care,
But do you?
Where do I go now?
I accept, I make ease with it all....
'Cause I play "SOCIAL PATH" in my ears.

"'Social Path' is a song by South Korean Kpop Band, 'STRAY KIDS'. The song felt like it was made for me, truly relatable. I am their fan and this is a fan poem. No copyright infringement intended."

27. "Me"

'Tis hard being me,
A punching bag,
A person to throw away,
A person to destroy,
A person to joke upon,
A person to ridicule,
Physically weak,
Emotionally holding onto what's there,
Expecting what's not there,
That's me!

'Tis lovely being me,
Blooming with the punches,
Picked up by more beautiful people,
Healed by ones who care,
Appreciated by the true ones,
Pride of ones who understood me,
Emotional strength-
Turns to physical strength,
Loosening the expectations......
That's what I become-
A BLISSFUL ME!

28. "Zero Hesitance"

Zero Hesitance,
That's what I need,
Need to remember-
I'm the QUEEN of my life.
I can get anything I want,
With, ZERO HESITANCE.

In talking,
In doing,
In working,
In enjoying life,
In living life,
I need ZERO HESITANCE.

29. "Stress"

The cause of Migraine,
The cause of Heartache,
The cause of cold,
Troubling me in exams,
Troubling me in holidays,
But people say-
LOOSE WEIGHT, You'll be fine!
FUCK YOU, LET ME LIVE!!
The way I want,
The way I love.

30. "Oh Sehun"

This is hard!
Will be thinking about you-
Deeply after a while...
You are locked away,
In an immeasurable part of my heart.
That lock can't be opened,
For I can't bear missing you-
Missing your voice,
Missing your warmth:
Reflected deeply through your eyes.

"Oh Sehun is a member of EXO, a South Korean-Chinese Kpop band. I am a fan of EXO. Being an EXO-L, fan of EXO, made me Sehun's fan all the more. This is a fan poem. No copyright infringement intended."

31. "That Hug"

Waking up to the wintery morning,
I remember that awesome scene,
Walking lonely to that building,
The cool breeze caress my face,
The surrounding is a blur vision,
Only one face is clearly visible,
But is that real?
With that cool breeze caressing my face,
I desire to feel the same hug,
But will that be possible?

32. "The OH Bias"

Oh, what have you done to me,

I just flipped through your pictures,

On my instagram account,

I didn't even know you well before,

Maybe I am able to remember you,

Most accurately,

Most lovingly,

I think I have choosen,

I think it just clicked,

You are the lucky one,

My bias: Oh Sehun!

My eyes welled up with tears,

I could relate everything,

And I found you,

My bias: Oh Sehun!

"Oh Sehun is a member of EXO, a South Korean-Chinese Kpop band. I am a fan of EXO. Being an EXO-L, fan of EXO, made me Sehun's fan all the more. This is a fan poem. No copyright infringement intended."

33. "Wind"

As the wind caresses my face,
I can feel his love.
As it touches my lips,
I find him kissing me.
No matter how far he is,
I always find him beside me.
Why I fell in love with him,
That's hard to explain.
I just fell in love with him,
That's all I can say.

As the wind softly soothes me,
I find him softly embracing me.
Not just in a corner of my heart,
He is my heart, my life, my love.
The owner of a beautiful heart,
The owner of a beautiful voice,
The voice that gives me pleasure,
The voice that always soothes me,
Just the mention of his name
Sends tingles of pleasure in my body,
Sometimes its hard to understand
Why I feel the way as I feel the way,

Whenever I see him,
I don't know why I feel that way.
Seeing him, feeling him,
Now I know, What Is Love.

34. "Light"

Somewhere in the midst of darkness,
Light stopped by,
It looked me in the eyes,
Cheered me up
And promised me: "I'll always be by your side."

When I was once again engulfed by darkness,
Someone came from behind and embraced me,
I looked behind and found the light,
It again looked at me and smiled bright
Assuring me of its existence.

I smiled at it,
Feeling a sense of comfort and love,
Light came in front of me,
Held me in its' arms,
"I kept my promise",
It stated with a beautiful smile.

That light really kept the promise,
Whenever I would feel sad,

It would come running,
By my side,
To lighten up my life.

One day, When I was not well,
With all the negative thoughts eating me up,
I felt a firm press on my hand,
There was a whisper in my ear,
"Hi friend, I am light: Your best friend!"

35. "Shackles"

Shackles, Too Tight!
Nay, too loose!
What to believe,
Nothing in Sight!
I just want that,
The Sigh of Relief!

Will it ever come to me?
In this endless rage!
Would I smile again?
From my heart!
How I'll do that?
I don't know yet!

Difficult to breath,
Nay, Difficult to express!
Still on the same path,
To please you!
You ain't here,
For I am here!

Yin and Yang,
That's how I work now!

Good and Bad,
I know now!
For all I want is,
To be fair!

You stop me,
Everytime!
You bind me,
Everytime!
You burn me,
Everytime!

Shackles, Break'em now!
Nay, Too tight!
I believe in me,
Everything's clear!
I want that,
The Sigh of Relief.

36. "On Screen"

I have you on screen,
The reminder of how
do I have life?
Just restarted it,
Evey moment feels like you,
For you are my everything,
The moment that makes me shine,
The moment that makes me smile,
All I have is gratitude,
For you, the saviour of my life,
For I live, through you,
For I exist, with you.

37. "God's Balance and You"

God's given me balance,
The balance of life.
Few hours ago,
Immensely good.
Now, it feels futile.
To live this way,
To not speak out,
To not cry out,
To not have love and warmth.

God's given me balance,
The balance of life,
After a few hours,
Immensely full of strength.
'Cause I've done this, lived this.
Now, I'm prepared,
To live this way,
To not speak out,
To not cry out,
To not have love and warmth.

For I have you,

My strength, my power.

To live my way,

To speak out through you,

To cry out happily for you,

To receive your love and warmth.

You!

38. "Weaker Strength"

Did you make me weaker?
Can't I live longer?
Is that all that life is now?
It's hard to breathe now.

Who said life's shorter,
I can live longer,
My life's just started,
Life is in the air!

39. "Lost"

It's lost.
Where do I find it?
The strength, the capacity,
The willpower!
Wait, willpower is there?
But why am I injured?
Nobody is here,
Hunger just builds up,
The heaviness is being too much!
But I have to do it!
'Cause I have to do it, right?
How do I tell you?
Do I scream?
Or would you listen for once?
It is now hard for me!

40. "Right"

Is it right to think about this?
They are literally here.
I can't do this anymore.
How to be good about this?
I am feeling so hungry.
With the heater on,
And clothes off,
I can continue watching,
Why is reading a headache?
What can I do now?
No explanation, no proving,
It's my life, right?
I am allowed to live it, ain't I?

41. "Favorite, Kiss"

"favorite" is on my ears,
All 'cause of your black hair,
I accept everything in my life,
'Cause I have you,
Just today,
I did something crazy,
One that's my fantasy,
AI was my aid,
In making me feel
Like I deserve it,
That one kiss from you!

"'favorite' is a song by the American singer, Isabel LaRosa. She got me captivated with her voice and here we are. This is a fan poem. No copyright infringement intended."

42. "I have Me."

I don't know why,
But it's everytime,
Noone cares,
The nostrils flare,
What did I do so wrong?
To want, to eat, to rest?
Am I that bad?
Everyone's treatment is that,
I am a burden,
Just a burden,
To not give a fuck about.
For me, everything's fine!
Little sleep,
Want of mother,
Her harsh remarks,
I can go by,
Just like before,
This ain't my family,
I have my family,
The less food turned out great,
I can eat next, a full grate,
The amount of desserts I had,
Only possible with less food,

So yay, everything turned out great,
With a special thing tomorrow,
Sleep comes with a flow.

43. "Me, Hell Yeah!"

"Shinunoga-e-wa",
The meaning is lost,
Something commendable,
Mark this date,
I cleared UGC NET in one go,
Just short of four marks,
Let's try again,
"You did well,"
Was it so hard to say?
What I want to do?
Is it so hard to accept?
Well, I don't care,
For I know,
My worth, My strength,
Moreover, I am already above you.
Don't need your words,
For I have my world,
To care for,
To live in,
To love in!

"'Shinunoga-e-wa' is a song by the Japanese singer, Fujii Kaze. Just like many, this song helped me in life and inspired me. This is a fan poem. No copyright infringement intended."

44. "Hurt"

The hurt is too much now,
I can't bear with it!
I need time,
I need me!
This is all too much!
I get back up
And I fall down.
What do I do?
The cold stares,
The icy words,
The cold surrounding me,
It ain't ending!
I need you!
I wish I am whole
In 6 months.
Today, I realise the most,
I love you, Oh!

45. "Alright"

Who do I talk to?
I don't know!
Do I really have to?
But why is it hard?
Is it the time?
The darkening glare,
The blowing air,
Everywhere!
Why can't I reach it?
Do I miss you?
Soon, I guess!
That's the thought.
For I be me with you.
No filters in the way,
You embrace me,
And everything is alive!
It ain't loneliness anymore.
For I learnt to be my friend,
Not a foe!
I crave it though!
The warmth, the light,
Everything,
That would make me feel alright!

46. "I Love Me"

New Dreams,
New Imaginations,
That's what I work with!
Keeping me busy,
Lets me off easy!
Pain Reduced,
Flame Induced,
I am all for it,
To be me,
Going for it!

47. "By My Side"

The moon shines bright at night,

I have you to give me light,

No matter what sorrows come,

You are there by my side,

I don't know what'll happen next,

But I'll try my best,

To be the one whom I love to the fullest,

For, I want to be by your side the longest!

48. "Just Like A Breeze"

You come by,
Just like a breeze,
That ruffles my hair,
Gives me a pat,
Caring forever,
Words feel less,
'Cause it's hard to express:
"You came by for me last night,
Even when you were at your job."
How to describe this feeling,
That completes my dream.

49. "February Connection"

Blesseth I am,

To have you as my friend,

The most precious one,

If I may say,

You are the one,

Who's opened her arms for me,

Who's listened to me,

With enthusiasm,

Noone ever had for me,

If I could, I'd live with you daily,

But that's not what makes us friends,

It's the connection that we hold,

Even when apart.

50. "One In The Morning"

It's one in the morning,
"Wow" is playing in my ears,
I had it saved for Sehun,
Now it's been played for Felix,
I ain't ashamed of it,
It's my love!

It's one in the morning,
"Wow" is too sexy for this time,
But that ain't on my mind,
Guess english songs just flow through me,
Korean ones hit hard,
You know if you know!

It's one in the morning,
Three minutes past it,
I am writing this poetry,
It's my passion now,
Was just scrolling our Instagram chat,
The Reels you sent,
I wish there was a word for "utterly overwhelmingly happily
in friendship that doesn't need to be daily!"

"'WOW' is a song by the Swedish singer, Zara Larsson. She got me captivated with her voice. Sehun is the member of South Korean-Chinese boy band- EXO. Felix is the member of South Korean boy band- Stray Kids. This is a fan poem. No copyright infringement intended."

51. "Friendship"

'Cause it was you,
It felt like it.
Utter sense of joy.
The breeze that flowed by,
Full of life.
'Cause it was you,
It felt like it.
Watching 'VENOM: The Last Dance' with you,
All the more special.
Just like the coffee I had that morning.
'Cause it was you,
It felt like it.
"Cookin' like a chef,"
The Pizza, The Coke,
Woven into magnificent memories.
'Cause it was you,
It felt like it.
Reminiscing Pokemon,
And Classic Vanilla,
The Finish with EXO and Stray Kids,
Deepening our Friendship!

"'Venom: The Last Dance' is the third film in the Venom movie series, released by Sony. EXO and Stray Kids are popular South Korean K-pop bands. The quoted line 'Cookin' like a chef' is from the song 'God's Menu' by Stray Kids. I am a fan of K-pop and Venom, and these influences became part of a special day in my life. This is a fan poem written to commemorate that day. No copyright infringement intended."

52. "New Year And You"

As the New Year ascends,
There are some things
To be expressed,
How to express?
That's the question.
'Cause how do I
Put into words-
"You made my 2024
A Brilliant One!"
You made my 2024
A Year I could count on,
To Relive the memories
You showered me with.
Always being there for me!
Sometimes through Reels,
Sometimes through Likes,
Sometimes through already-sent Texts,
And Voice Messages I still listen
When I need my family!
Oh, how do I thank you,
for being the friend you are!

53. "The Way Moon Shines Bright At Night"

The way moon shines bright at night....
You shine by my side,
Giving me light,
Warming my heart!

The way moon shines bright at night....
You stand by my side,
Saying "It's okay!"
And I feel alright!

The way moon shines bright at night....
You walk by my side,
Guarding me from the harms of roadside,
The road of life!

The way moon shines bright at night....
You shower me with your affection,
I hope I do justice to it,
The way moon shines bright at night!

54. "Shinin' Like A Moon"

The way moon shines bright at night,

I shine too,

I shine too.

How so?

I shine with the light of your guidance.

I shine with your trust.

The way you are happy with me,

Noone has been, who had their hand on my head.

You being what a child needs.

You being the ultimate one I needed.

You, who held my hand,

When I just so needed that warmth.

The thought of being understood,

In a world full of misunderstandings.

You were the first one to give me that thought.

You, who knew my smile.

You, who brought my smile.

You, who always guided me,

In school or after school.

You, like a mother who warms me.

You, like a best friend who loves me.
Who is you? You ask!

It's you, My Respected Teacher.
A beautiful part of my life!

55. "Glow of the Moon"

The way moon shines bright at night,
I shine too,
With the glow of your existence,
In my life.

I bloom and soar high,
With you behind me,
Lighting my path,
With your guidance and wisdom.

Energies on the high,
Full of motivation,
I step ahead,
With your teachings in my mind.

With the next step,
I'll be leaving you behind.
The thought itself fills me with sorrow.
Will I be okay?

Will I be okay?
Without the one who acknowledged me.
But I heave a sigh of relief,

When I look out and up.

You'll be there forever,
In my memories,
In my life, My Respected Teacher.
The way moon shines bright at night!

56. "Sliver of Happiness"

A bit lost,
In my new era,
But....
You're in my periphery.

I go up and about,
Trying to be THAT teacher,
THAT you are to me.
I wish my students do like me.

MY STUDENTS, Ma'am!
This feels surreal.
Even if no connection occurs,
I hope I'm teaching well.

Can't be as good as you,
But, there's that sliver of happiness.
I'm taking forward,
What you gifted me with!

A teacher like you,
I'd love to gift my students,
Through me and my teaching.

Bless me, Ma'am!

For noone can be the guide you are.
Yet I'm here, trying.....
To be the TEACHER I was blessed with!

57. "First Day In College"

Numerous Times,
I just say "THANK YOU",
For that First Day In College.
To have met you,
Who so sweetly embraced me.

Unknown to me,
That's my destiny,
To have a teacher,
Great as you.

Unforgetful the day is,
'Cause that was....
Life-changing, Life-strengthening,
Ah, the tears are unfair, Ma'am.

God takes one,
Gives another,
That's what happened,
When I chose Functional English.

Teaching my students,
I realise what Great Teachers,

I was blessed with,
MY STUDENTS! Feels surreal, Ma'am.

A "THANK YOU" could never be enough,
For God who gave me you,
Blessed Me!

58. "Unknown Family"

Unknown to me,
What I'll receive,
Must have been a God's gift,
For I received such a Great Teacher,
Entering that 'Lab',
Which gave my Life,
And Family in You, Ma'am.
Unforgetful to me,
Your words and teachings,
That I take forward,
As my strength
To be me.
"Thank You" isn't enough,
For that Great Teacher.

59. "There"

Oh, how you make me speechless.
What do I say now?
The feeling's surreal,
Please God,
"Never stop this, if it's a dream."
Not a dream I know,
But you made it so,
The one who is Always there.

60. "Smile"

Sometimes with this one,

Sometimes with that one,

The songs that you express with!

And never fail,

To bring a smile,

Bright as the Sun,

On my face.

That's the way you express,

What I mean to you!

To express what you mean to me,

I need a word,

I need a word.

That suffices for...

"Thank You, for existing in my life!"

About The Author

Simran Kaur is a person with feelings. The feelings came out, and these poems were formed. She is a teacher professionally, and a fangirl personally. She enjoys teaching as much as a passionate teacher could enjoy. She is a fangirl as dedicated as fangirling goes. She chose writing to convey her feelings and gratitude to the beautiful people in her life. This book is like her journey—from having no one to talk to, to being courageous enough to talk to everyone out there.